P9-DXL-257

CALGARY PUBLIC LIBRARY

NOV - - 2012

Written by Loris Lesynski   Illustrated by Gerry Rasmussen

CRAZY ABOUT SOCCER!

annick press
Toronto • New York • Vancouver

PHOTO BY BABAK

For
Wendy Marion Cecil,
someone who really
moves

—*LL*

© 2012 Loris Lesynski (text)
© 2012 Gerry Rasmussen (illustrations)
Design & Art Direction by Loris Lesynski, Laugh Lines Design

Annick Press Ltd.
All rights reserved. No part of this work covered by the copyrights
hereon may be reproduced or used in any form or by any means
—graphic, electronic, or mechanical—without the prior written
permission of the publisher.

We acknowledge the support of the Canada Council for the Arts,
the Ontario Arts Council, and the Government of Canada through
the Canada Book Fund (CBF) for our publishing activities.

ONTARIO ARTS COUNCIL
CONSEIL DES ARTS DE L'ONTARIO

Cataloging in Publication
Lesynski, Loris
    Crazy about soccer! / Loris Lesynski ; art by Gerry Rasmussen.

ISBN 978-1-55451-422-9 (bound).—ISBN 978-1-55451-421-2 (pbk.)

1. Soccer—Juvenile poetry. I. Rasmussen, Gerry, 1956-
II. Title.

PS8573.E79C73 2012   jC811'.54   C2012-902100-8

Distributed in Canada by:
Firefly Books Ltd.
66 Leek Crescent
Richmond Hill, ON
L4B 1H1

Published in the U.S.A. by
Annick Press (U.S.) Ltd.
Distributed in the U.S.A. by:
Firefly Books (U.S.) Inc.
P.O. Box 1338, Ellicott Station
Buffalo, NY 14205

The artwork in this book was done in pen and ink and Photoshop.
The poems are set in Chaparall Pro. Titles are in Bryan Talbot Lower,
with page numbers in Shake Open, both from www.comicfonts.com.

Printed in China

Visit us at: www.annickpress.com
Visit the author at: www.lorislesynski.com
        or www.crazyaboutsoccer.ca
Visit the illustrator at: www.gerryrasmussen.com

You can write to Loris
c/o Annick Press, 15 Patricia Avenue, Toronto, ON M2M 1H9 Canada
or e-mail her at LorisLesynski@gmail.com

BOY OR GIRL
SOCCER
BRAIN:
brilliant
always on

SOCCER EYES:
see everything
everywhere

Water in:
LOTS
breathing in
and out: LOTS

SOCCER ELBOWS:
very bendy

SOCCER
ARMS:
as fast as
propellers

SOCCER SHOULDERS:
strong!

SOCCER
HEART:
crazy in
love

SOCCER HANDS:
no fingerprints on
the ball

SOCCER STOMACH:
full of nutritious
power food

SOCCER KNEES:
very necessary

REAL GRASS

SOCCER
FEET:
essential,
fantastic

FAKE GRASS
(turf)

All in the Ball

Take away the uniforms,
 take away the cleats.
Take away the cheering crowd,
 take away the seats.

Take away the referee,
 take away the net.
Take it all away today—
 right away—and yet—

We'll always have a game to play,
 positions for us all.
It isn't in the extras.
 The game is *in the ball.*

Crazy About Soccer

muscles deflated
legs like spaghetti
cleats full of mud
exhausted and sweaty
sometimes a good game
sometimes the worst
we're tired and grimy
and dying of thirst
but back here tomorrow?
you bet
and we'll play
day after day after day
after day!

Soccer Simply Everywhere

ANYTHING
can be a net.

ANYTHING
can be a ball.

ANYONE can
play the game

ANYWHERE
at all.

Kick a Ball...
Kick a ball in Holland,
kick a ball in France.
Kick a ball in Egypt
if you ever
get the chance.

Kick a ball in Canada,
kick a ball in Spain.
Kick it from the USA
to China and Ukraine.

Kick a ball
around the world,
kick it in the street.
Kick it anywhere
you've got
a soccer ball
and feet.

7

How Soccer Started

The game began so long ago,
    exactly how, we'll never know,
but one day someone said, "I've found
    that kicking things along the ground
is really fun, and if we get
    it in those bushes like a net,
it gets a point! And getting more
    is how we win—we'll call it SCORE!"

They tried some rules that very week,
    invented starting-up technique,
and made up moves, and cleared the pitch,
    but still there seemed to be a glitch.
It could have ended then and there
    if someone wise had not declared:
"*This* is why it goes so slowly—
        soccer needs a
            smaller goalie."

Did Shakespeare Play Soccer Between Writing Plays?

In Shakespeare's day, the people played
on cobbled streets, in fields of hay,
up mud roads and down in ditches—
no such thing as proper pitches.

Hardly any rules at all.
Anything could be a ball:
chopped-off head, or piggy bladder.
Good equipment didn't matter.

Homemade boots instead of cleats.
Bloody, brutal, fierce defeats.
Matches played from town to town,
knocking one another down.

For centuries a lasting game.
It's good to know it's stayed the same.
Well, *some* of it, but no, not all—
I'm glad we have a modern ball!

How Soccer's Different from Other Sports

Some sports are played in water.
Some sports are played on ice.
("Never get the two confused"
is excellent advice.)

In many games, the uniform
will tell you who supplied it.
Some have so much padding, it's
a secret who's inside it.

Many sports have clubs, or bats,
or sticks to hit the ball.
Goggles, helmets? Skates and masks?
They have to have it all.

You won't believe the stuff you have to
buy for other sports!
All we need are shoes and socks
and jerseys.
Oh, and shorts.

In soccer, your equipment
is your body and your brain.
Add a ball, that's all that's ever
needed for a game.

Soccer in the Future

a hundred years from now, will they
be playing soccer like today?

perhaps they'll have a match on Mars
and soccer stars will play *with stars*

new inventions, new machines
will modernize the moves and teams

they'll find a way to harvest watts
from energy in soccer shots

to light the earth, and all for free
as soccer electricity!

cleats with engines?
balls with jets?
only robots at the nets?

play a game or two someday
with someone half a world away

future changes—let them come!
nothing's going to change the fun!

Striker's Job

React? Now.
React? *Quick.*
React? *RIGHT?*
React! **KICK!**

First-Touch Chant

the FIRST touch
is much
more important
than **ALL**
of the other
techniques
used in
handling
the ball

•

the **FIRST** touch is much more
important than
ALL of the other techniques
used in handling the **ball**

•

the**FIRST** touchis**MUCH**
more**IMPORTANT**than
ALLoftheother
techniquesusedinhandling
THE BALL

FOR BALL

WHAT A GREAT BIRTHDAY PRESENT!

Soccer Sense

you *know*
the ball

you understand

exactly where
it's going
to land

what makes it
fly

what makes it
soar

exactly how
to make it

SCORE!

Throw-In

The other team
thinks
that I
intend
to pass it *left*
so they'll
defend
the shot
that way.
But hey!
That's *not*
the way (AHA.
it really goes—
the ultimate
in phony throws!

Foolery

adding trickery
to your kickery—
is it sportsmanlike
or sneakery?

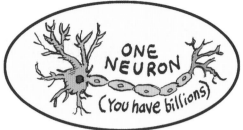

ONE NEURON (You have billions)

Messages Don't Get Any More Instant Than This!

It's hard to believe there's **TIME** at all to **THINK** before you shoot the ball.

It's hard to believe there's **TIME** at all to **PLAN** before you pass the ball.

It's hard to believe there's **TIME** to **PICK** exactly where you aim a kick.

BUT THERE IS!

It Went Here, It Went There...

If balls
left all
their moves behind
in markings or
a dotted line—
what a tangle!
weird and crooked!
what a mess
the field would
look-ed!

Soccer Balls, Big and Small

Soccer balls come in
a number of sizes,
some small as donuts,
some wide as pie-zes.

The First and the Second
are small souvenirs.
The Third one's for children
from four to eight years.

Up to age twelve, kids'll use
Number Four.
Then Five is the biggest,
what pros use to score.

Suppose someone tried out
a brand-new design—
imagine a *header* with
Ball Number Nine!

BENDING the Ball?

You can't bend the planet,
you can't bend the air,
you can't bend the ball
to make it go where
you want it to go
even though
someone did.
Beckham's the envy
of every kid.

The Power of Suggestion

I hinted at it...
mentioned it...
and gave a lot of clues.
A dozen times, I said that this
was just the gift to choose.
My hinting's so terrific,
when at last
my birthday came,
I got the one
I wanted—
and a dozen all
the same!

Seven Nine Six...

(**796.334** IS WHERE SOCCER BOOKS ARE FOUND IN EVERY LIBRARY)

There are tons of books on soccer
with instructions and advice.

I get them from the library
and some I've studied twice.

But learning how to play like this
is cutting down my speed.

I have to find a better way
to run and also read!

Soccer 'Round the Clock

time for bed
but in my head
it's **SOCCER!**
SOCCER!
SOCCER!
in my sleep
I keep
on kicking
SOCCER!
SOCCER!
SOCCER!
can't take the time
to stop and rest
my soccer moves
must be the best
I love it!
YES
I am obsessed
with
SOCCER!
SOCCER!
SOCCER!

Warm Muscles = Oomph

Muscles half asleep and cold?
Stretch and hold. Stretch and hold.
Little holds, no bouncing yet.
Feel how warm they start to get.
Twist and *turn*, jump *up*, jump *down*.
Have a little runaround.
Warmed-up muscles stretched and loose?
POW! What power they'll produce!
Ready, strong! Alive and roaring!
Doesn't *matter* warm-up's boring.

Muscles here,
muscles there,
I've got muscles everywher
(even in my smallest toe)
they're what make me
stop and go
warming up before I play
GUARANTEES
a brilliant day!

WO

But We CAN'T Stop!

Joking causes trouble
  and our kicking starts to wobble,
and we muddle up the moves
  the team intended.

  But when we get the giggles
    in the middle of a dribble,
  we could *laugh* and *laugh* and *laugh*
    until suspended!

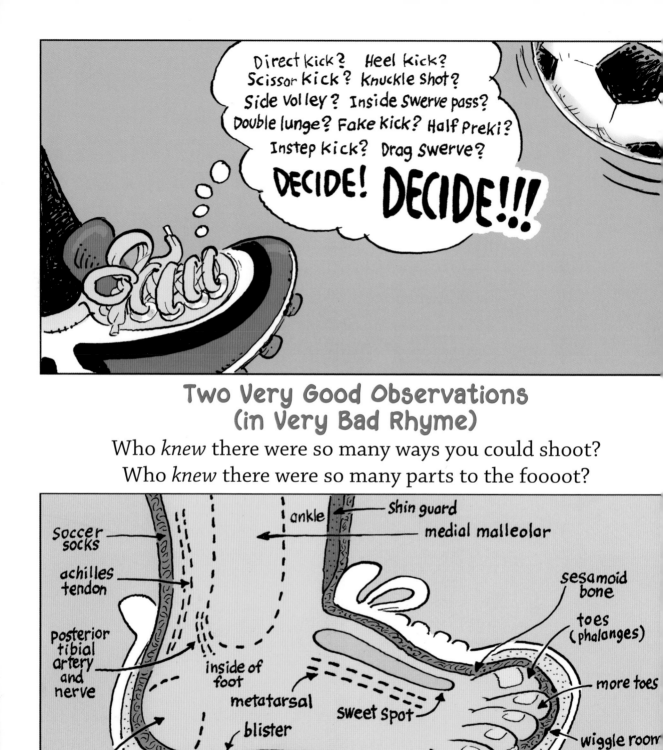

Two Very Good Observations (in Very Bad Rhyme)

Who *knew* there were so many ways you could shoot?
Who *knew* there were so many parts to the foooot?

'Cuz They's *Important!*

so, i thought, before soccer,
that feet was just feet,
    i didn't know "angles" and "zones"

feet was just muscles
and fat and toes
    and a coupla useful bones

but no—feet for *soccer*,
she says, says our coach,
    are special in plentya ways

it's cool if you know
what to do with them so
    you can make some spectacular plays

they gotta be quick,
   for a killer kick,
and put up with stops and starts

  so get 'em good cleats,
and protect them feets,
   and train every one of them parts

No Favorites!

One of my feet is fantastic,
    powerful, nimble, and free.
It feels like the ankle's elastic,
    but locked when I need it to be.
The other foot's floppy and dozy,
    and just wants to watch TV.
If they're planning on playing soccer,
    they better decide to agree.

Why Tigers Aren't Allowed on the Team

Tiger, tiger, shooting past
the rest of us, so sure and fast.
Passes with his big back paws,
dribbles with those skillful claws.
Sure, he gets a lot of goals—
but now the ball is full of holes.

XXXXXXXXL

If an elephant played soccer,
he would need a jumbo shirt,
and he'd leave behind a crater
every time he hit the dirt.

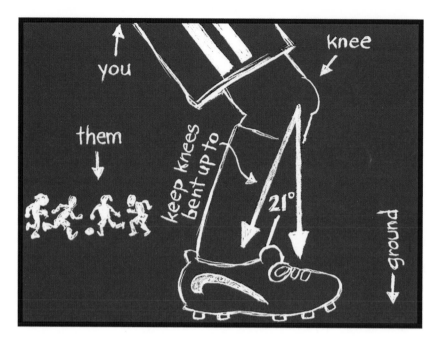

We Need Knees!

fat or skinny,
smooth or hairy,
knees are very
necessary.

soccer's most
important joints
(it's not just feet
that score the points).

Ronaldinho says that knees
bent up to 21 degrees
are always ready, knees that know
exactly where the ball will go.

knees be nimble
knees be quick
knees I need
a perfect kick!

Pick Up Those Knees!

"Pick up your knees!
Pick up your knees!
Juggle the ball
with precision and ease
Pick up those knees!
They don't get to stay
in the same old position
all day today."

What does he mean?
Is the coach insane?
Knees *ARE*
where knees *ARE*—

he better explain.

KangaKicks

Anyone
 at all,
 at all
can learn to kick
 a ball,
 a ball.
A kangaroo
 could do it,
 too,
a bigger kick
 than me
 or you,
but never put one
in a game
'cuz they can kick—
 but
  they
   can't
    AIM!

Arms Set the Pac[e]

Soccer scientists
  say this is true:
as fast as your arms go,
  your legs will go, too.

Most people think
  it's the other way 'round,
that feet set the speed,
  from their place
on the ground.

But no, it's your arms.
  Even though they're bann[ed]
(from the shoulder down
  to the end of your hand)
from touching the ball,
  it's arms that decide
the fast or slow
  of your running stride.

Way Too Pointy!

An elbow is not a weapon!
Would somebody tell Jerome?
Tell him he has to obey the rules—
or leave them both at home.

Red Card to Humpty D.

Humpty Dumpty wasn't just
"relaxing" on the wall.
Humpty had been benched because
he tried to crack the ball.

Rain Game

coach says we're on,
and won't let us complain

but face it, a game
in the rain is a pain

we try to keep playing,
we shoot and we pass

getting wetter and wetter
and skidding on grass

my shin guards are soaked
and so are my shins

rain defeats cleats

slippery wins.

The trouble
with sliding?
COLLIDING!

How to Be a Referee

Want to be a referee?
  Get ref education.
Memorize the rules for
  every soccer situation.

Go to reffing classes.
  Take the ref exams.
Learn to analyze about
  a zillion diagrams.

The whistle: never swallow.
  Daydream? not too much.
Notice every single foul and
  kick and pass and touch.

And what's the most
  important thing
you learn at
  reffing school?

Knowing how,
  no matter what,
to **NEVER**
  lose your cool.

What the Ref Sez Goes

everybody knows
what the ref sez goes
what the ref sez goes
kinda useless
to oppose him
what the ref sez goes
'cuz the ref is in control
over every single goal
over kicks
over throws
so from little kids to pros
it's what everybody knows
what the ref sez goes
what the ref sez goes

Height? *Ha!*

The grass is short, and so am I
    but when I move my feet, they fly.
Soccer balls don't care at all
    if kicked by someone short or tall.

Soccer Suggestion

I'd be a better player
    if I had a few more feet.
The two I've got are not enough
    to make a pass complete.

Beginners' bikes have extra wheels
    to give them more control.
I bet some extra feet
    would guarantee
      another goal.

Peripheral Vision

Isn't it amazing that
    no matter what I'm gazing at
my eyes can see so much outside
    the center spot—in fact, so wide
I know where all my teammates are
    including near, including far
across the field. I see with eyes
    like brilliant little soccer spies,
ahead and on the sides of me
    and all of my periphery.

Soccer Eyes

soccer eyes
see all around
they're on
the ball
they're on
the ground
they keep
a watch
on high and low
and always know
    where kicks
        will go

SORRY!

Please Please Please No Injuries!

mud and blood
a bad combination

somebody made
a miscalculation

seems that kicks
don't always land

- exactly where
the kicker planned

Beginner

I'm starting
to look like
an eggplant,
purpler every day.
Nobody chooses
this many bruises
except when
they're learning
to play.

Turf Burn

turf burn turf burn
can you say it fast?
turf burn turf burn
pain that's gonna last

plastic grass can really
scrape you
coach is going to have to
tape you

wonder *why* they'd
want to make
a soccer field
so good a fake?

(in the spring,
the robin's wish'll
be the *worm's* not
artificial)

The Concussion Discussion

Have it!

GLUG GLUG GLUG... *AHHHH!*

Hot and dizzy in the sun?
Scorched before the game is done?
Drink some water! *Now*, no waiting.
You might be EVAPORATING!

Drink that water all the time
and always drink a lot of it.
Drink it sooner, not too late—
don't wait 'til you've thought of it.

If your insides get too dry,
you get so tired, you could cry—
and crabby, too! Your mood's the worst
right before you die of thirst.

Goalkeeper, Goalkeeper

Goalkeeper,
what do you need
to succeed?

Instant reactions?

Acceleration?

Automatic
coordination?

Know every rule
of a violation?

Make every guess an
exact calculation?

We asked all the coaches,
the coaches agreed:

WHAT GOALKEEPERS NEED

is

SPEED!

The Dive at the Net

There's no way their ball's getting into the net.

This season, not *one's* gotten past him yet.

He starts like a statue, in Goalkeeper Stance.

When will he leap? Does the shot have a chance?

He's got to start low, staying square to the ball.

He plans how he'll leap and then cushion his fall.

And it's on, his fabulous daredevil save!

As sudden and fast as a tidal wave!

Sideways and forwards and back all at once.

We've watched him in practice for months and months.

He drops to the ground, and all of us scream.

From down in the dirt he grins up to the team.

We win once again, now it's three in a row.

And that's why we call him Tornado, not Joe.

We Lost Today

We're brokenhearted.
  We're totally sad.
We lost today.
  We feel so bad.
Coach is checking
  every bruise.
We need some Band-Aids
  for the blues.
    And then some ointment
    for disappointment.
    Nobody,
      nobody,
        NOBODY
          NOBODY
feels any good
    when they lose.

How to
Never Lose
Another Game

Never play one.

Why I'm Quitting Soccer

love the game *SCREECH* love the ball.
like the coach, my team and all
but gotta give it *SCREECH SCREECH* up
because i *hate*
the whistle!

i can't *bear* it, can't be *near* it!
never *SCREECH* know
when i'll hear it
or how many
SCREECH SCREECH times—
like insanely screaming chimes.

my whole nervous system's shot
OW! my ears! and *SCREECH* it's not
too good at all for *SCREECH* my brain!
but coach says *SCREECH*
when i complain
"Just be a sport and tolerate it."
doesn't know how much i hate it!
SCREECH the squealing
SCREECH so shrill
how it hurts! can *SCREECHES* kill?
i have to quit and find a *SCREE-EEECH* sport
without
a whistle.

"Header" Variations

They call a ball a "header,"
when it bounces off your head.
But what about a ball that lands
on somewhere else instead?

Want to try a "noser"
or a "cheeker"
or an "earer"?
Either hide, or *quick*, decide—

the ball is getting
nearer!

43

Now Invite Some Zebras to Play, Too...

If you're black and white all over,
and the room is just the same,
it might not be the perfect place
to play a soccer game.

What's black and white
and black and white
and black and white and black?

A penguin rolling down a hill
the ball behind his back.

Soccer Camouflage

We're Crocodiles, starting a brand-new team.
The coach ordered jerseys and shorts all in green.
Who knows how we play? We can hardly be seen!
Next season, let's be
Flamingos.

Moon Ball

late one night this summer,
it was so hot, we lay on the grass
outside the house

the moon, it seemed,
slipped down for a while
to become our ball
we passed it with bare feet
and sent it to one another
in the shadows of the garden,
the only sounds
the crickets,
some cars far away,
the thumps of our kicks,
and our laughing:
    we were playing soccer
    with the moon!

      or maybe we fell asleep

but the next night, we saw them,
    the little dents on the moon
      where we'd touched it
        with our toes

Want *more* soccer poems?
Write some of your own!
Find out how at www.crazyaboutsoccer.ca

More stories and collections of poems by Loris Lesynski

www.LorisLesynski.com